IRENE WILSON

'THE CINDERELLA MEDIUM'

IRENE WILSON WITH RICHY HORSLEY

www.warcrypress.co.uk
Richy Horsley (c)

978-1-912543-10-6

The Cinderella Medium ISBN: 978-1-912543-10-6: All rights reserved. No part of this publication may be reproduced or transmitted in any form or by any means, including photocopying and recording, without the written permission of the copyright holder, application for which should be addressed to the publisher via the dealing agent at: warcrypress@roobix.co.uk, such written permission must also be obtained before any part of this publication is stored in a retrieval system of any nature. This book is sold subject to the Standard Terms and Conditions of Sale of New Books and may not be re-sold in the UK below the net price fixed by the Publisher / Agent.

The Cinderella Medium Produced by www.wacrypress.co.uk (part of Roobix Ltd: 7491233) on behalf of Richy Horsley, Hartlepool. Copyright © Richy Horsley 2018. Richy Horsley has asserted his right as the author of this work in accordance with the Copyright, Designs and Patents Act 1988.

Cover Photo by Wendy Horsley

Printed and bound in Great Britain by Carter & Jackson, Pontefract.

Find out more at: facebook.com/warcrypress

AUTOBIOGRAPHY OF A SPIRITUALIST MEDIUM

FOR MY IMMEDIATE FAMILY

AND MY SPIRIT FAMILY

CONTENTS

1 THORNLEY

2 THAT CINDERELLA FEELING

3 I'LL NEVER LEAVE YOU

4 BARE ESSENTIALS FOR THE LITTLE MOTHER

5 CHANGING TIMES

6 THE GYPSY SAW TRUE

7 THE MINERS STRIKE

8 INTRODUCTION TO SPIRITUALISM

9 THE MEDIUM

10 THE SEVEN PRINCIPLES

11 BACK FROM THE DEAD

CHAPTER 1
THORNLEY

I was born in December 1943 during the Second World War in a little mining village called Thornley in County Durham. My parents were living with his father, my Grandfather Routledge.

In 1943 we had a hatched, matched and a dispatched as they used to say. My grandmother Routledge died in the April, my parents were married in the September and I was born in the December.

Grandfather Routledge was a First World War veteran and a stickler for discipline and ruled the roost in the house but my parents were grateful to him for taking them in. They lived in the bedroom, slept in the bedroom and ate in the bedroom. I suppose a lot of families did that back then. They kept their food in orange boxes that were pushed up against the wardrobe.

My parents Edward Routledge and Catherine Griffiths (Eddie and Kittie) were childhood sweethearts and went to the same junior and senior schools. They both left school at 14 and dad went to work at Thornley Colliery as a miner. Mam went to Skipton in Yorkshire to work at Dr Barnardo's for orphaned children were she stayed for three years, only coming home during the holidays to meet up with dad.

On 11 September 1943 they were married at Easington Register office at a cost of five shillings (25p in today's money), a small fortune in those days but laughable today. You could do a lot with 25 pence in them days; it won't even buy a bar of chocolate nowadays. Mother wore a coat made out of an old army blanket. Food and money were scarce and everything was on ration. Hardship was everywhere. Being whisked off to an exotic location on honeymoon was a world away back then.

Mam was pregnant when dad went off to fight in the war in 1944 so she moved in with her parents, my granda and grandma Griffiths. There were eight of us living in a three bed roomed house as my grandparents still had children living at home. War ended in 1945 and my dad came home and moved in as well to take the tally to nine and then mam was pregnant again. Everyone had large families back then, if you asked anyone what contraception was they wouldn't have a clue.

I remember my mam and grandma Griffiths washing in the back yard using a poss-tub and stick, it was a hard laborious domestic chore that most women usually done on a daily basis. Sometimes when the coal man had delivered the coal outside the back door and us little ones had been playing in it and got as black as soot, we would be put in the poss-tub to be washed clean.

My parents got a house right opposite my grandparents so we only moved over the road. It was a terribly harsh winter that year, one of the coldest on record and it snowed that heavy it stopped all the traffic coming in and out of the village. Dad had to do the errands to the bakers for bread and to the milkman. He got his job back at Thornley Colliery after coming out the army and worked long hours at the pit just to feed and clothe us.

Thornley grew pretty quickly in the 1800s with the development of coal-mining in the region. The first shaft was sunk in 1835 and the first coal was delivered shortly after by a new railway line to Hartlepool. The village played a major role in the development of Hartlepool as a port. The colliery closed in 1970 with the loss of 900 jobs and there is little evidence left of the once extensive plant and machinery.

We had a good family community around us when I was a child and we all lived in close proximity. Everyone was in the same boat so to speak; we all had nothing and all leaned on each other. All the men worked down the coal mine, the kids went to the same school and the mams looked after the home and the babies. People who grew up in a community like that learned to trust and love each other. They didn't take kindly to strangers coming in but they accepted them.

My two times great-grand parents were Welsh miners and when the mines were opening in the North-East they came here because there was plenty of work. They were staunch Methodist and it was passed down on my mother's side to me, my brothers and sisters. Every Sunday afternoon my brothers and I (my sisters weren't born yet) had to go to chapel from two o'clock until three. We used to have a card that would be stamped with a blue star to prove we had been. The only reason I had to stop going was our family had grown so much that I had to help mam in the home and do the Sunday dinner. I missed going to chapel and loved singing the hymns and listening to the stories about the prophets and Jesus.

I suffered with tonsillitis as a baby and seemed to get infections easily. When I was four I came down with pneumonia and had it for two months and almost died. I remember laying in a white-cot with vertical railings and I don't know if they were white in those days but the one I was in was white. I remember being above the cot and looking down at myself laying there and the doctor came in and I heard him say "oh bloody hell the needle has snapped," after he put it in the muscle in my leg.

The doctor had to go back to his surgery (which luckily wasn't far away) on his pushbike and get another needle. While this was going on a woman all in white appeared to me and said:

"You can't come over here, you have to go back."

The doctor came back with a new needle and injected me and I heard him say to my mother "she is going to be alright," and when he said that I woke up.

When I told them that I saw everything that happened and repeated their conversation, and that the doctor had to go and get a new needle because the other one had snapped, they were open mouthed in amazement. That was certainly an out of body experience I have never forgot and the spirit world have been quite active with me for a long time.

I used to sit under the table in the kitchen with my dolls and talk to them. I still remember my mother saying in a loud voice:

"Stop talking to yourself or you will end up in the looney bin."

Those words would be repeated quite often and even my mother's friends used to warn her to tell me to stop talking to myself or I would end up in the loony bin. They didn't know but I was communicating with spirit from an early age and they would show me different things when I was sat under the kitchen table, I wasn't talking to my dolls like they thought I was. I learned to keep my mouth shut about spirit communication because mam would have taken me to see a psychiatrist.

I had suffered quite a lot with tonsillitis so when I was in my teens the doctor decided it was time for me to have them removed and I had the operation at Dryburn Hospital in

Durham. I was in there for ten days and made some friends and chatted to everyone who came in. I used to help the nurses make the tea and hot chocolate every night. There was an older nurse who was a very caring soul and she told me I would make a good nurse if I chose that profession.

When I recovered from pneumonia I started Thornley infant school. My grandma Griffiths took me and I don't know who was upset the most, me or her. I remember her telling me to be a good girl as she turned and walked away.

Thornley was a happy place and everybody knew each other and all the kids went to the same school except the catholic families; who went to a school of their own on Wheatley Hill road, but we all grew up together and played together, games like kick the tin, two baller, hopscotch, knocky nine doors, skipping ropes and other games of the day. You had to get outside and get a bit of sun when it came out because winters were very long and harsh.

Some winters were memorable when we made snowmen and had snowball fights and dad made a sledge what we had some great fun on. We would take it to the top of the bank and bomb down on it feeling like you were going one hundred miles an hour, the thrill in your stomach and the freezing cold air on your face was magic.

A couple of times we went down to Hartlepool for a week and stayed at an Aunts house for a bit of a holiday. You can get there in ten minutes by car these days but nobody had a car in back then and the bus journey would take an hour and a half, stopping at every bus stop on the way. Once we arrived at our destination at the united bus station we still had a long walk ahead of us through street after street, and through the industrial estate, and dad would be saying 'come on it will do you good' before finally arriving at the house in West View. We slept on blankets on the bedroom floor with no luxury of a mattress but we enjoyed ourselves.

I remember going to Seaton Carew for the day with the family and lots of cousins. We set off on the bus at 8-30 am and didn't arrive until 11am, you can do it in15 minutes by car today. The first thing I remember seeing was the helter-skelter and I was feeling sick off the long bus ride and my cousins were all excited shouting 'look at all the shows.'

All the women had big bags full of pies, sandwiches, biscuits and cakes what they had made. Sandwiches usually had the customary sand in them after being on the beach.

We hired two huts, one was for all the babies and their things and the other was for everyone's bags with the food, towels, swimming cosies etc and we'd be swimming in the sea having great fun.

"Go over to that van and get a bag of winkles" said dad. Then, when we were eating them our older cousins would call them 'snots in crash helmets' and it put me off eating winkles. The lads would play cricket on the beach and we'd also play with a tennis ball and racket and everyone had a great time. We'd stay there all day and get back home about 8-30 pm, great memories.

One day my father came home with a piano what he bought at the furniture shop in front street, he said he wanted to learn to play it, whatever for I don't know. Anyway I was the one who learned to play it. I was sent to Mrs Armstrong's every Friday at 5 o'clock to learn the piano and it cost two shillings a lesson.

Mrs Armstrong played the organ at St Bartholomew Church of England church in the village.

Our school had a talent show for all the local talent and I entered it. I played 'The merry wives of Windsor' on the piano and got second place. I received a certificate and felt very proud. First place went to a girl called Janice Muir who was a ballet dancer.

I had been going to piano lessons for a couple of years and I had learned to read music and lots of other things. I would practice as much as I could at home and Mrs Armstrong said I should go in for my exams and I started studying for them. Little did I know then that my studies would all be to no avail.

My father bought a television and it opened up a whole new world for me. I stopped going to piano lessons because the times I was supposed to go was the time my favourite programme, The Cisko Kid, came on. I loved that programme.

"Two years paying for piano lessons and she's packing it all in." said mam.

Well they shouldn't have bought a television!

Sometimes we would go to the matinee at the local cinema on a Saturday afternoon and it was threepence entry. Mam would wash out the empty jam jars and we would take them to Stan Cook's little fruit and veg shop down the street and he would take the empty jam jars off us and swap them for bruised fruit that wasn't on ration like pears and apples. Really good days and great memories but things started to change for me as I started to get a little older.

CHAPTER 2
THAT CINDERELLA FEELING

Mam had child after child and each year brought another mouth to feed. She had thirteen children and with me being the oldest, more and more responsibility lay on my shoulders. There wasn't another girl born until mam had her sixth child so I was expected to help out but the work load everyday became harder and heavier.

"God put you on this earth to help me look after the children" mam said that to me so often that I ended up believing her.

While my friends were out playing, I would be indoors helping mam with the ironing, washing, get the children ready, scrubbing bare floor boards in the bedrooms, we didn't have carpets but we had clean floors. Once a fortnight I would empty the stuffing out of the pillows, wash and boil the covers, re-stuff the pillows and sew them back up because we didn't even have pillowcases.

Mam would say different little phrases and one of them was 'cleanliness is next to godliness.'

The neighbours would call in and say 'you can eat meals off these floors' and they weren't far wrong. It was hard back breaking work and it went on every day, week in week out, month in month out and year in year out. Every day was Groundhog Day.

"Put other people first Irene and you won't go far wrong." mam's words seemed to stick in my head.

Some mornings I would be woken up by spirit. A voice would wake me up saying 'hurry up or you're going to be late' and if I hadn't listened to the voice I most certainly would have been. I had all the children to feed and get ready before I could get ready and go to school. We had a big cast iron pan that I called a cauldron and I would make the porridge in that every morning. I felt like Cinderella but even Cinderella had it easier than me.

Dad worked every hour god sent to feed and clothe his brood which was constantly growing and we didn't see much of him because of it, but he liked to go out on a Saturday night with his work mates, usually to the dog track. Mam didn't mind him going out because he worked so hard.

Every Saturday it was my job to clean out the fire and polish it. I would clean all the ash and cinders out and black lead all the fireplace. I would put the black paste on to a cloth and rub it on all over then leave it for twenty minutes and rub it over again and it would come up like a shiny new pin.

One Saturday mam told me to get the polish out and polish the lino as well which I did, we didn't have carpets back then, only rich or posh people could afford them. Then mam put an imp up the chimney which we did once a week to keep the soot from blocking the chimney because it would make the house smell of coal if you didn't. I always remember the tin had a little impish devil on the lid.

Well this Saturday a huge amount of soot came rushing out and blew the bleezer off the fire, a big heavy steel bleezer that was made down the pit, and in shock I started screaming and there was clouds of soot everywhere.

Mam came running into the room and shouted 'where are you' and I said 'I'm over here', you could only see the whites of my eyes and I was literally covered in soot.

Once I got clean, I went over the road to my grandma's and said 'can I borrow your hoover grandma', it was just a handle that went down with a cloth bag and motor on and my god it was heavy and the noise was like a big old tank. I always remember her saying in her bit of Geordie twang 'what does thou want with me hoover?' and when I told her she said 'you've got a silly mammy haven't ye' and we both laughed.

The soot was that thick around the fireplace and on the lino mam told me I had to clean it all again. I remember grandma chuntering as she went out the door 'I'll wash me hoover down and empty the bag. I can't believe she's making a kid do two jobs like that.'

My grandma didn't like the way my mam used to treat me with all the chores I had to do it was like having a full time job. Dad used to say to me 'just do what she tells you and complain after,' which I couldn't get my head round because I thought you complained before!

Dad always had a nice calm temperament and I can't recall him ever losing his temper. Mam on the other hand was a different kettle of fish. Only 4ft 11in and fairly well-built, she had a hard life and woe-betide if you got on the wrong side of her!

I liked bed time because it gave me that time and peace to be by myself, even though the other children would be laid beside me they would be fast asleep. Now and again in bed I would silently ask God why I was sent here in the first place and sometimes I would cry myself to sleep. As strange as it might sound, but when each new day dawned I would thank God for another day even though I knew nothing would be any different.

When I was eleven I went to the 'big school' which was Wheatley Hill Girls Modern, the last school I would go to before I went out into the big wide world. I was pretty proud of myself after leaving my junior school in Thornley and going to the senior school in Wheatley Hill, which was another mining village which took about fifteen minutes to walk. I know this because my school friends and I walked it every day.

On your first day you had to do an exam to see if you went into A or B class. To my surprise I went into 'A' which was the top class. The only subject I struggled with was maths but the teacher said I would pick it up as I went along. I had never heard of algebra or fractions.

It was an all-girl school and the teachers were middle aged, old fashioned and opinionated. My maths teacher was a well-made spinster called Miss Hope and she had a hefty slap on her which made your ears ring for a week. One day she asked me to say my nine times table and I would always get stuck on seven times nine and could never remember it. She shouted at me and made me feel like an idiot in front of the whole class, she would do that on more than a few occasions. When I would take my book to her to get marked and if I got any wrong, she would throw my book to the back of the class and embarrass me. She said to me:

"When you leave school don't go for a job in a shop because no one will employ you."

Years later I wished I could have met her and taken her back to those words she said because I bought my own shop and ran it by myself. At the time though it played on my mind and I would pray at night to be put into 'B' class.

Then one day the headmistress sent for me to go to her office and when I went in she told me I was being moved down into 'B' class. It was then that I started to enjoy school because I wasn't getting anxious about my next maths lesson. It didn't matter to me one little bit who was top or bottom because in my eyes everyone is equal.

On the walk home from school my friends would ask me if I was playing out and I was never able to give them a yes or no because I never knew what mam wanted me to do that night, so I'd ask them to call for me. Sometimes I was allowed out but most of the time I wasn't. It was as if I wasn't allowed to make my own mind up and mam was letting me know who the boss was.

I remember my thirteenth birthday when I got my first ever birthday card and it was off my grandparents. I opened it and there was a ten shilling note inside and grandma said I could spend it how I liked. I was so excited I felt sick. I read the verse and just stood there and cried and grandma gave me a big hug and said 'you soft lump' with a smile on her face.

I never got to spend the ten shillings on myself because my mam's needs were greater than mine so I gave her it to help her out and she told me not to tell grandma.

One time when grandma Griffiths said she and granda were going to Redcar Horse Races on Saturday and asked would I like to go with them, I looked at mam and she said yes straight away which surprised me but I would have to do housework first!

I did the usual morning chores and also cleaned the windows and helped prepare the dinner and then I was off.

It was raining so I wore a wool coat with a pixie hat. I had knitted the pixie hat with the help of mam's sister, my aunt Joan, who taught me how to knit when I was six years old. My grandma wore a wool coat too and a little black hat with a hat-pin in to keep it on. My granda wore his best suit with a white shirt and a tie and looked very smart.

We got the 11 o'clock bus and the journey there was long and boring but I remember going past the steelworks at Middlesbrough and asking granda why the fire out the chimneys floated in the air, he just looked at me and laughed.

Grandma had baked meat pies and home-made cake the night before and she put them in a shopping bag for the trip. We ate them on the bus because the grass was wet from the rain. There were thousands of people there, I'd never seen so many people in my life, all shouting for their horse to win and my granda did win one and gave me sixpence to have a ride on the shuggy boats. I was sick when I got off.

On the way back home everyone on the bus seemed to be very happy and singing and I was excited to be with my grandparents as I loved them to bits.

I always felt spoilt with my grandparents and I knew they loved me because I could feel it in abundance from them. My granda always called me 'Dot' because I was six pounds when I was born and he said I looked like a skinned rabbit.

They used to go to Blackpool in the summer for a holiday in the 'pitman's fortnight' when everyone would break up from work. They took me with them a couple of times when I was little. Not once did I ever hear them argue or fight, they were lovely grandparents and the love just flowed from their hearts.

My grandma was my role model in life, she never smoked, never drank, didn't tell lies, she was about 5ft 5in tall and around fourteen stone. Her laugh was very contagious and when she laughed everybody laughed with her. What an incredible woman and nothing seemed to bother her.

I remember when they took me to Blackpool and we stayed in a lodging house, these days they are called Bed and Breakfast. I got up the next morning and went to the bathroom but when I opened the door a man in a pair of blue and white striped pyjamas was stood there staring at me. I got the shock of my life and shut the door and shouted for grandma. She arrived asking what was the matter and I told her about the man in the bathroom and I wanted to go to the toilet, so she knocked on the bathroom door and shouted 'Open the door' and there was no answer. So she opened the door and there was nobody there!

Grandma said "There you go again seeing things."

That man could not have gotten out the bathroom without coming out the door and I was stood outside it; so I knew the man wasn't a real person but someone you would term a 'ghost'. I remember my grandad saying to me: "Don't worry about it pet my mam was just like that and it looks like you take after her."

Our school was going to Edinburgh for a day trip and before I asked mam if I could go I knew the answer would be no, anyway as look would have it my grandma was sat listening and said:

"Why can't she go?"

"I can't afford it," said mam

"I'll pay for her to go" said grandma

I felt little flutters of excitement in my tummy.

"When you come out of school tomorrow night; meet me in the CO-OP and we'll get you something new to go away with" grandma said.

She bought me a new pair of shoes and socks and a lovely two-piece jacket and pleated skirt, the height of fifties fashion. It was light blue and I loved it. I was thrilled to go on a train for the first time and Edinburgh was like being in another world, Princess Street and Edinburgh Castle and then to the Zoo. It was all magical to me and I loved every second of it.

Although I had a hard life helping mam there were still some happy times in my childhood like the ones I've just mentioned and another one was when I was bridesmaid at my aunt Joan's wedding when I was eleven.

Aunt Joan was mam's younger sister and she wanted me to be a bridesmaid which I was thrilled about. It was Boxing Day 1954 and there was snow on the ground, it was a white Christmas and picture postcard weather and scenery. I wore a beautiful long blue satin dress with a flower garland in my hair and carried a basket of flowers. My shoes were slip-ons like what a ballerina wore, I looked lovely and I felt like Cinderella at the ball. What an amazing day that was.

CHAPTER 3
I'LL NEVER LEAVE YOU

It was time to start thinking about what I wanted to do after I left school because it wasn't that far off and you know how fast time goes. I thought about my own beliefs, I knew about God and I was here because of him but I wanted to go further into it. I really wanted to know who I was, what was my purpose here and where was I going from here. I didn't know then that I would become a medium.

"Stop talking to yourself Irene there is no one there, you'll end up in the nut house", I can still here mam say that but little did she know I wasn't talking to myself.

I thought about becoming a nun and had a notion about becoming a missionary and going overseas and helping people less fortunate than myself. I mentioned this to my mam and wished I hadn't.

"You can't be a nun you're not a Catholic" she said,

"So, I'll change my religion" said I,

Mam then started giving me a tongue lashing and I couldn't understand why.

Then I said:

"It's God's wish for me to help people in need and be charitable in life",

"Yes, but charity begins at home" she said.

Yet again another little bit of her philosophy crept in. I had no intentions of arguing with her so I just stayed quiet. I had never been cheeky to my parents and wasn't going to start now.

The thought of me becoming a nun went straight out the window but it didn't stop me sending healing thoughts and prayers to all the people who were suffering in this world.

Another thought came in my head, what about being a nurse? I had an idea about how to treat cuts and bruises but most of all I had compassion in my heart for other people. Yes that's what I'll be, a nurse. I sat and visualised myself in a nurse's uniform and it suited me fine but this time I kept it to myself and didn't say anything to mam.

I was in the school library reading a book about a young woman called Gladys Aylward who worked as a parlour maid to a rich family. She saved her wages up so she could go to China because she felt a calling to become a missionary. She spent her life savings just getting there but once there she worked with an old missionary called Jeannie Lawson and together they found The Inn of the Eight Happinesses. They provided hospitality for travellers and shared stories about Jesus.

In 1938 when they were invaded by the Japanese forces she led more than 100 orphans to safety over the mountains even though she had been wounded. I was engrossed in her story and wanted to be like this incredible woman. She never married and devoted herself to Christian work with the people of China and founded an orphanage. She became a Chinese citizen and was a revered figure among the people, intervening in a prison riot and was an advocate for prison reform. She risked her life on many occasions helping those in need. What a brave and unselfish person and her story stayed with me since that day I read the book.

One night after mam and I had just finished bathing all the children and had put them to bed we watched television and Eamon Andrews 'This is your Life' programme came on. When he announced who it was I gasped with excitement, it was none other than Gladys Aylward, I couldn't believe it. Some of the children who she saved came on including a boy who she carried all those miles who she called 'sixpence', and she never forgot about the young man who helped her and was shot by the Japanese. Gladys left an impression on me that stayed with me.

I went to bed that night and when saying my prayers I asked God why I couldn't do anything like that and within a couple of seconds I got my reply when I heard a spirit voice say 'Your mother needs you more.'

I started growing up and my body started changing which I knew nothing about as I was never told about it. I had noticed some girls at school had bigger chests than me but I was very naïve about anything like that, then one day mam said "we will have to get you a brassier". You could have knocked me over with a feather.

Even when I reached maturity I still looked like a small girl which had its advantages as I could still get on the bus for half price. It was also embarrassing at times like the time I went to the movies to see a horror film and you had to be sixteen to get in and I would be turned away because I didn't look old enough. I remember when I was twenty four years old and married with two children, my husband and I went to the local club for a night out and the doorman refused me entry because I didn't look 18! Luckily my husband convinced him I was old enough.

I left school at 15 and didn't become a nurse or a nun, instead I got a job at Paton & Baldwin's wool factory in Darlington. The works bus would pick us up at outside the Catholic Church at half past six every morning and we'd get to work by 7-15 for a 7-30 start. I made some good friends at the factory and we all got on very well.

Wednesday was pay day and I got £2-16s per week. Mam was over the moon with the extra pay packet coming in and I used to hand over my unopened pay packet to her every week and she would give me half a crown pocket money on a Friday.

I started as a bobbin girl because I was only 15 and not allowed on the machines until you were 16 and that's when I was trained to be a spinner, working the spinning frames I was taught how to spin wool to the finest knots. The bobbins of wool had to be perfect when spun because they were exported to other countries. I must say I took pride in my work and loved my job and was hardly ever off in my three years there.

15 February 1962 is a day I'll never forget. At 5 0'clock in the morning there was a knock at our front door and it woke me up. It was my granda and he asked if my dad would go and sit with my grandma while he went and got the doctor. I immediately sensed something was wrong and got up and went over to grandmas. I heard the doctor telling my granda and my parents that grandma had passed away and it was a heart attack. She was only 58. I could hardly believe what I was hearing and couldn't take it in. It was the most horrendous feeling losing the woman who I loved with all my heart. She was a lovely lady who would sit down with you and listen to all your troubles and always had time for you. Not only was she my grandma, she was my best friend and was more of a mother to me than my own mother. She gave me a meaning to

life and I loved her dearly. Her death affected me badly, I couldn't eat or sleep and when anyone spoke to me I wept.

The day before the funeral my aunt Rita took me upstairs to see her. She was laid in a coffin covered with purple and white satin. She didn't look like my grandma but I rubbed her cheek and kissed her and told her how much I loved her and missed her terribly. My aunt Rita said to me: "It's going to be hard for you but you'll get over it. It won't go away but you will learn how to cope."

My grandma's death had a great impact on me, although other people close to me had passed over, none of them had this effect on me. I didn't know it then, but saying goodbye to my grandma wouldn't be the last time I would see her.

A few weeks later I was washing my hair in the sink, I'd wet my hair with a jug of half cold and half warm water and wash it and then rinse it off with a jug of half cold half warm water. I'd just finished rinsing my hair and wrapped the towel around my head and when I lifted my head up my grandma was stood in front of me. I got the shock of my life. She was wearing a lovely dress what I'd never seen her in before, it had a big white wide collar with a red rose in it and the dress itself was black, white and red with cap sleeves and red roses on it.

We exchanged a few words and I said:

"Have you come back?"

"No I haven't," she replied, "I want you to stop crying because I'm alright and I'll never leave you."

Then she was gone.

I'll never forget those words and they gave me so much comfort.

Mam was knitting in the sitting room and heard me say 'have you come back' and knew I was on my own so came to investigate and said "Who are you talking to?" and I replied "I've just seen my grandma". Mam thought I was having delusions and told me to get something to eat and drink.

My aunt Joan came to the house and I relayed to her what happened. I told her about the dress that grandma was wearing and her eyes widened. It was then I found out that the week before my grandma died; she had bought herself that exact dress but hadn't had a chance to wear it and it was hanging up in her wardrobe. I didn't know anything about her new dress and hadn't seen it; all I did was describe what she was wearing when she appeared to me.

Seeing my grandma made me realise she wasn't dead but was very much alive and had only 'moved on' to somewhere else, another existence were you don't need a physical body because you are spirit and it gave me so much comfort to know that.

That night I had a 'dream' that I was leaving home. I didn't know where I was going but I was watching myself walking along a road and heading off to a new village to start a new life.

I didn't know, but before I headed off, life was about to get much harder for this Cinderella.

CHAPTER 4
BARE ESSENTIALS FOR THE LITTLE MOTHER

Around six to eight weeks after grandma passed to spirit, my mam took to her bed and wouldn't get up. We thought she was just missing her mam (my grandma) but dad thought we had better get the doctor to check her out. I walked to the surgery and asked for the doctor to come out and see my mother and the receptionist said he'll come when surgery finishes at 2pm. When I got home I told mam that the doctor was coming to see her today and as I walked out of the bedroom I heard a knock at the front door. When I opened it there stood a little Romany Gypsy woman wearing a long brown wool coat and she had a scarf around her head, her face was weather worn. To me she looked like a North American Indian. She had piercing blue eyes that looked like they were going to cry, but it was the cold. I recall she had black suede boots on with a zip up the front and one of the zips was broke. I was shocked and she seen the look of fright in my eyes and with a kind smile said 'hello'. I just stood looking at her and not wanting to be rude I said 'hello' back. It then dawned on me that this was the lady known as 'Gypsy Rose' who would come knocking on people's doors when the fairground came to Thornley and as you guessed, the fairground was here. I'd been to the fairground as a youngster with my grandparents but never as I got older because my mam wouldn't let me go with my friends.

Gypsy Rose would tell people their fortunes for gifts, money, tea, coffee, sugar or any other gifts people offered. People believed if you didn't offer anything she would put a curse on you.

She said: "My name is Gypsy Rose and I'm not here to frighten you."

She asked if she could tell my future and I said no because I didn't have a thing to give her in return. She said 'it doesn't matter' and started telling me I would be free of the burden of everything that was going on in my life, looking after all the family etc and I would marry someone called Joe and have three children and be happy. She said "Is your mother poorly in bed," and I said "yes."

She said: "There is a decision to make, whether to put her in hospital or put her somewhere else for rest because she needs peace and quiet."

I was nearly crying with her accurate message and told her to wait while I went inside and I got her a packet of tea which I gave to her and said thank you, she was over the moon with the tea and gave me a little pixie charm as a gift.

She also said to me:

"Don't tell all what you see."

I didn't understand that until later when I learned to 'keep my mouth shut' about the spirit people I saw and the images I would see and the voices I would hear.

The doctor diagnosed mam as having a nervous breakdown and reckoned it was the death of her mother that brought it on. He wanted her to go to Sedgefield where she would get the quietness and attention she needed but mam wouldn't go and wanted to stay home and be nursed, so I packed my job in at the factory to become a non-paid housemaid. I was 18 years old, had no Job and no life to speak of and if I thought my life had already been hard it was about to get a lot harder.

Mam was sedated for the first ten days and it took three weeks for her to be able to sit up in bed. My day would start at 6am and everyday was washing day, then after getting the bairns fed and watered and off to school I'd be stripping the beds, washing the windows, scrubbing the floors, making the fire, making the meals, Ironing, doing the errands to the shop for bread and milk and potatoes etc. It was never ending.

Remember there were fifteen of us in our house and I was looking after everyone. We didn't have much but we had a clean house with plenty of home-made food. The neighbours knew how hard I had it and used to call me 'The Little Mother' while others called me 'Cinderella'.

Fifteen would soon turn into sixteen when my brother's pregnant girlfriend moved in. We didn't tell mam because she was in bed poorly and probably wouldn't have reacted very well to the news but the girl's parents were adamant that my brother David faced up to his responsibilities and married his girlfriend Iris. David had gotten a job at Thornley coal mine and Iris was from Wingate and there was no way he could get from Wingate to Thornley pit for work because there wasn't the transport, plus her dad said they didn't have the room, so they moved into our house which wasn't far from the pit.

Four weeks later David and Iris (both 17) were married and I was a bridesmaid. Her parents paid for everything, it was a nice quiet wedding with the tea at her grandparent's house but my dad and I couldn't stay because we had to get back to see to the children and to my mam.

A few months after David and Iris' wedding I started to get tired and weary. The non-stop heavy workload was taking its toll and it started to get on top of me and I told my dad that I thought I might be coming down with something.

I started hearing voices. I had heard voices before but they were more frequent now and I was seeing shadows. We had a dog that died of old age and not long after he died I was serving cups of tea and I saw the dog lying under the table. I told the dog to get in the kitchen and my dad asked who I was talking to and I said the dog that's lying under the table? Dad said "Irene the dog died weeks ago," and I had totally forgot about that because I saw a real dog lying under the table. It was a bit like getting engulfed in a fog and becoming highly sensitive and I could 'feel' and 'see' spirit people telling me things and started to 'hear' whispers in my ear.

They say you have to go through hard times to appreciate good times and I don't really know why my mam treated me differently to all the others. I felt like she hated me because of how she treated me and I would never treat another human being, or animal, like that. She was a tyrant to me and never once did she tell me she loved me and not once did she ever hug me. I'd be cleaning or doing housework and she'd shout "make me a cup of tea" and not once did she ever say please or thank you. Once when I took her a cup of tea to her bedroom she threw it back at me because it was 'too strong'. I don't want to sugar coat this and looking back on it now I was a 'slave' for want of a better word.

I remember once when one of my brothers had left his coat on the floor in front of the fire and as I walked past it I stepped over it. Mam who was sitting in the armchair knitting, noticed I stepped over the coat and said: "Pick that coat up instead of stepping over it" and I replied "It's not mine" and she picked her cup of tea up and threw it at me! I ducked and the cup missed me and smashed the sitting room window!

"Look what you have made me do now. Wait till your father gets home from work you'll get it" she scowled.

My uncle Jack came round and removed all the broken glass and put some wood over the window. He was laughing but I didn't think it was funny and when dad came home he didn't say much just his usual "Do what she says and complain later." Dad was always peace itself and anything for a quiet life.

My dad and I found out the main reason for her nervous breakdown. When mam became poorly and the finances had to be worked out, there was more money going out than was coming in. Dad wanted the debts paid off so we introduced austerity measures and cut back on most things apart from the bare essentials, there were no luxuries. It was very tough but we managed and eventually it paid off.

I didn't realise until I was married and had three children of my own what hardship my parents went through and I only had three kids not thirteen. My childhood has made me a stronger person and in a way I have mam to thank for that, but it isn't nice when people dominate others, especially children like she did with me, because they think they know best. Some do it out of ignorance and some think they are bringing them up morally and proper. I personally think children should be heard; after all they do have rights and opinions of their own. In my own case I did not. It was a case of speak when spoken to, sit there and move nothing but your eyeballs and I obeyed because I thought mam knew best. I grew up shy and introverted and wasn't very good at making conversation and it always seemed everyone was more knowledgeable than me. When I started work in the factory at fifteen I struggled to mix at first, but after a while it got better as I got used to people and got to know them better. I always say 'we are all strangers until we meet' and I made friends that I keep in contact with to this day.

One day in the autumn my cousin Margaret came to the house and asked me to be a bridesmaid at her wedding the coming December and I said yes. I told her in private that I didn't know where I would be as I could feel a big change in the air. She told me she wanted me on her wedding photographs and I said I wouldn't let her down. I always loved weddings, they are such happy occasions. I had always been the bridesmaid and never the bride and when I saw how beautiful our Margaret looked in her wedding dress, I wondered if one day I would ever be lucky enough to be the bride.

Mam was starting to get over her nervous breakdown and said to me:

"As soon as the reception is over you must come straight home. You cannot go to the club on the night."

I felt so disappointed and didn't argue with her and went home like she said. When I got home I found out I was baby-sitting because mam was going to the wedding party with my dad. A quick recovery from her breakdown!

Mam started going out more and more, not only during the day but at night as well, while I was home doing the housework and keeping it all together. She was depending on me quite a lot to do everything and it was taking its toll on me and I was becoming depressed.

One Saturday my Uncle Bob and Aunt Rita called and asked if I would like to go to the club with them to see Bobby

Thompson, a well-known comedian, and I stood up from sitting on the couch and collapsed.

It's hard to believe these days but back then they used to have a machine outside the shops that sold aspirin in long strips, about tuppence a strip, and I bought six strips and swallowed the lot!

I was delirious and could hear people talking but couldn't see them and Uncle Bob picked me up and took me to the toilet and made me put my fingers down my throat and be sick, which he made me repeat again and again. He made me a cup of tea and went ballistic with my mother and shouted at her and was saying things like "Look at the state of her and it's your fault."

Luckily I recovered and was fine but it was a cry for help and mam knew then that I'd had enough.

CHAPTER 5
CHANGING TIMES

Remember when I saw the 'ghost' in Blackpool and my granda said I took after his mam, my great grandmother. Her name was Emma Griffiths and I was her first great grandchild but she took to me like I was her grandchild. She came from a little mining village called Penshaw Moor and she was only 4ft 9in tall and was a size 2 in a shoe. I was only 5ft myself but I actually thought I was tall when I stood next to her. They say big things come in small packages; she was a little dumpy woman but what an incredible woman she was. She wore long black dresses and a lovely clean white pinnie which covered all her front. I remember her saying to her husband Enoch, who she had seven children with, "God forgive thee Enoch."

I recall she would stand at the gate and wave at me as I went past on my way from school and she would shout "Are you coming round?" and I'd shout "I'll come round when I get my jobs done."

When I would go to her house she would tell us ghost stories from when she was a little girl. Things like how she would see ghosts coming through the walls and things like that; it used to horrify me but my cousin Joyce must have been of a nervous disposition because she would be out the door like a shot. Once I got used to her she would say things to me like:

"I know things about people. I can see people from spirit that others called 'dead' people."

I stopped being scared and became intrigued by my great grandmother.

She had a neighbour called Mrs Lock who was her good friend and sometimes she would say:

"I'm going to Mrs Lock's tonight are you coming?"

I would say "No" but she would insist "Come on I know you will enjoy it."

Mrs Lock used to tell peoples fortunes and give them messages from the spirit world.

Great grandma Emma knew I was with spirit because she could see it and she would say to me:

"You will be doing this one day you just mark my words."

I'd go with her to Mrs Lock's bungalow and we'd set the fire away and put the bleezer up and we'd turn the lights out and sit round the table in the dark. My god I could feel lots of energy in that room and when the table started to moved I was blown away by it. Great grandma would say to me:

"If you hear a voice; don't worry about it you'll be alright."

Sometimes I would pop in with my school friends and great grandma Emma would wind them up. She had a pot that the lid didn't fit properly and she'd say "Did you hear that. He's at it again." And my friends would be out of there in a flash. She had a bubbly personality and was great fun as well. Good memories.

A couple of my friends asked if I fancied going to the 'Wheatley Hill Hop' on Friday night. I said they should ask my mother because if I asked her she would say no to me. Anyway my friends asked her and she said yes as long as I was home for such and such a time.

We got there and it was a shilling entry fee and there were live Rock n Roll bands on and everyone was bopping away, it was fantastic. Fashion changed and all the girls wore big flared skirts with starched petticoats which made the skirts swing round when dancing. The lads wore drain pipe trousers, long jackets with velvet cuffs and collars, blue or black suede shoes and boot lace tie and were known as 'Teddy Boys'. I had never really had a life outside the home but I loved my nights at the hop and made new friends, one girl in particular who I hit it off with on my first night was also called Irene.

The following Monday there was a knock at the back door and when I opened it there stood Irene. I said "How did you find out where I lived?" and she said she thought she would have a ride over because she had nothing to do, so she got the bus from Horden and when she got off she asked someone who pointed her in the right direction.

Irene worked shifts at the wool factory in Peterlee and was on earlies that week. She said she would be back over on Friday to go to the hop and was I going? I told her to ask my mam and she said "Can your Irene come to the Wheatley Hill Hop on Friday with me I'm getting the bus over from Horden."

Mam said "Of course she can."

Mam was as nice as pie with everybody else apart from me, I found very strange but there you go. Anyway that's how Irene and I became good friends. One night in our house my cousin Ray came in and Irene said to me "Wow, I didn't know you had a cousin that looked like that!"

"Do you fancy him like," I said

"Oh god yes he's lovely," she said.

Romance soon blossomed and they started seeing each other and fell in love. Ray was in the Army and stationed in

Germany and when he came home he would spend his time with her and after a few months Irene said they were getting engaged at Christmas.

When Ray was in Germany, Irene would stay over at ours some weekends and asked my mam if I could stay over at her house and she said yes. So the weekends at hers we would go to the 'White House Hop' which was great, there wasn't any live bands just records but it would get packed out and we always had a brilliant time. One night we had just arrived back at Irene's house and her brother Brian had five or six of his mates in and they were playing poker around the kitchen table. I looked in the mirror and I saw one of the lads but he wasn't looking at me, he was concentrating on the poker game, and a little voice in my head said 'I'm going to marry him'. I knew were the voice came from, it was from spirit and I felt a little shudder because I knew it was real. He looked like the singer Billy Fury.

In bed that night I said to Irene:

"I'm going to marry that lad who was sat in the corner with the mousy/ginger hair,"

"Joe Wilson?" she said,

"I don't know what his name is but I'm going to marry him," I said.

"Get to sleep you're round the bend." came her reply.

The next time she saw Joe she said to him ever so subtly "Will you take Irene to the pictures Saturday night she fancies you."

That was how our courting started but it didn't start well. He took me to see a film called The Mummy and I was bored to tears with it and munched my way through popcorn and sweets and drinks and felt like I was a stone heavier on leaving. He said "Did you enjoy the film?" and I said "No."

The next time we went out was when Ray came home from Germany and we went as a foursome down to the cinema in Hartlepool to watch a film called Zulu. I didn't like Michael Caine so I thought it was another bad film choice but I went anyway. When the picture came on, the scene was Zulu's doing a tribal dance and the women had nothing on their tops and Joe said to me:

"Do you know what that dance is called?"

"No" said I,"

"The mating dance," he said,

"I hope you don't think you're getting fresh with me," I said.

Then Irene piped up and said to Joe "You are lucky you didn't get her elbow in your face there!"

Irene and Ray got engaged at Christmas and when he went back to Germany she asked me to move in and I said "I haven't got a job so how can I."

Anyway I moved out of my parent's house and into Irene's and got a job at the wool factory. We had lots of laughs and I made new friends and I actually got paid and this time I didn't have to hand my pay packet over. I gave Irene's mam her lodge money and the rest was mine although I did miss my brothers and sisters, Irene also had a big family so I fit straight in.

Joe wanted to see more of me and it was becoming a problem because I was out with Irene all the time when Ray was away and I felt a bit torn between the two and not knowing what to do.

One Friday my mother turned up at the house and handed my baby sister Jacqueline over to me and said "She's missing you," and I replied "She's not my baby,"

"I know she's not but they are all missing you and want you to come back home, "said mam,

"They will be missing me because I did everything for them and practically brought them up" I said.

She turned the water works on and started crying. I knew she was trying to play emotional blackmail with me but when she left I was naturally upset because it was on my mind. She only wanted me back home to do all the chores.

A while later I can't recall how long maybe a year, I was having difficulty with Irene and Joe because both wanted me to go out with them all the time. I couldn't end it with Joe because I knew I was going to marry him, so Irene and I had a falling out because of it. It was difficult at work and being around her at home so I told Irene's mam that I couldn't go on like this so I was moving back home.

Her dad said "We've felt the tension for a while and if you think it's the right thing to do it's up to you."

Her parents were lovely people and I have some great memories of them but Irene fell out with me.

I went back home and got my job back at the factory in Darlington.

It didn't take mam long to get back to her nasty ways. She didn't like Joe and told me I had to finish with him!

One day Joe turned up and mam said to me "What does he want,"

I said "He wants to see me,"

"Have your talk and tell him to get away," she said,

"No I won't. You will lose me again and that will be the end, there will be no coming back." I said.

I wasn't going to lose Joe.

Joe was always quiet and still is today, but when he would come to our house he would sit in the chair and my mam would never speak to him.

One Saturday night my dad came home from the club and said to Joe "I don't like you."

The next morning I said to my dad "What did you say that to Joe for?" and he said "Well he sits there dead quiet and never talks and always has a packet of tabs in his pocket,"

"Well he's a single working lad and has no lodge to pay, his money is his own, it's not his fault that we are the way we are. You have to work to feed and clothe 13,"

"I know I shouldn't have said that to him." Dad said.

When Joe came up the next night my father apologised to him and shook his hand.

CHAPTER 6
THE GYPSY SAW TRUE

Our Edie and husband Brian hired a caravan at Crimdon Dene for a week and asked me and Joe if we would like to go and we could help out with their children so we thought yes why not and went with them.

One afternoon we were sitting in the caravan having a cup of tea and chatting away and through the window I saw our Ray, he was stood on the green looking at me. I got a shock because I thought he was in Germany and I was just about to say to Joe, "There's our Ray what's he doing here," and something made me keep quiet so I spoke out in my mind:

"What are you doing here Ray?"

"You'll find out," Ray said and then waved goodbye to me.

Brian was doing his hair in the mirror and said to Edie "Here's your mother and father,"

I had a feeling what it was about and said "I have to go home,"

"You have to go home why?" said a bewildered Joe,

"Something has happened," I said.

Edie's parents told everyone the sad news that Ray had died suddenly.

I went to see Ray's parents. Ray had died in Germany, while out on manoeuvres, from a burst Ulcer; he was only 20 years old.

Irene was at the house and in a terrible state and we just talked and talked and she cried and cried. Ray was her life and she was totally heartbroken. My aunt got the doctor out to give Irene something to make her sleep because she was having a bad time coming to terms with the awful tragedy and was grief stricken. I felt for her.

After our Ray's funeral, Joe had asked me to get engaged and I told him he would have to ask my parent's permission first so he plucked the courage up and went to see my dad.

"I want to get engaged to your Irene and I'm asking your permission" said Joe,

"Only engaged, you don't want to marry her then," dad said,

"Yes but we want to get engaged first because we want to do things properly" said Joe.

After mumbling on and saying this and that dad finally said yes.

When he asked mam she said "No she's too young, wait until she's 21."

My father raised his voice and said "Kittie you just stop it or you'll drive her away," and mam said "Oh well please yourselves."

We went down to Hartlepool to a place called Scott's jewellers and in the window there were engagement rings for £3, this was the Christmas of 1963 and £3 for an engagement ring was a lot of money back then. When I got home and showed mam it she said "I don't like it."

I told mam I wasn't bothered if she didn't like it because it was mine and I liked it and I was happy. It was as if she couldn't bare to see me happy.

I mentally said to spirit "I've really had enough of it in this house please get me out of here".

I was still working full time and bringing money into the house, not getting home until 6pm and still doing the house work on a night.

I would talk to spirit a lot but not out loud and I could be in the room and see a spirit stood there and only I could see it. I remembered Gypsy Rose's words to me "Don't always tell what you see."

Joe knew that I could communicate with spirit but he was fine with it and it didn't bother him. Joe was a coal miner and worked at Horden pit, most of the men in the colliery villages worked at the pit.

On Saturday's I would go to his house and we would go out to the Sunderland pictures and places like that. I know you are waiting for the big marriage proposal now, him getting down one knee in the pictures before or after the big film, or maybe taking me out and surprising me with flowers and telling me he wants to spend the rest of his life with me because he can't live without me!

Well it wasn't exactly like that and my fairy tale proposal was a little bit different and not exactly what you would call fairy tale, in fact it wasn't even what you would call a proposal!

I was in bed one morning and said to my sister Joan "I feel sick," and Joan replied "You feel sick. What have you been eating?"

"Nothing, but every time I sit up I feel sick," and I kept laying back down trying to take the sickness feeling off.

"Go downstairs because if you're sick on me I'll hit you," said Joan. I knew she was only joking. Then a bit of panic set in her voice "Don't be sick on me Irene."

Up I got and down the stairs I ran, through the front room and out into the back passage way and threw up.

Later in the day mam said "Were you sick this morning?"

"Yes I had an upset stomach, I think it was the dumplings and mince-meat from last night," I said.

I had missed my monthly cycle, so a few days later I asked my sister Joan to come to the doctors with me. The doctor said:

"I see you are engaged,"

"Yes" said I; proudly displaying my engagement ring.

"Well you had better get married as soon as you can because you are pregnant" he said.

Our Joan's face was a picture when she let out a gasp.

As we walked home we called at the shop and got an ice lolly each and were thinking of how to tell mam and as we got closer to the house we could see her sweeping the yard.

"Just take your time I'm nearly finished" she shouted sarcastically. I told Joan I didn't know what I was going to say and she said:

"Just tell her the doctor said you are pregnant and if she has a problem with it tell her to go and see the doctor."

If it was as easy as that it would have been great but I was feeling sick, not with the baby but with the thought of telling my mother. We walked up the steps into the yard and mam was stood there with broom in hand.

"Well, what did he say?"

"I'm expecting" I said,

Crack!

Mother put the broom straight across my back and Joan grabbed it and took it off her and shouted "Leave her alone!", "She's having our baby leave her alone,"

I ran straight in the house and was quickly followed by mam who said:

"Here take these and run a hot bath and get in it,"

"What are these," I said

"They will get rid of the baby for you now get in a hot bath," mam said.

"I'm not doing that" I said and threw the pills in the fire and went upstairs out the way.

She shouted me down to help her with the dinner. It was my job to peel the tatties and we had a big family so it was like peeling them for an army battalion and they all had to be hand peeled. There is machines to do the peeling today but they weren't around then.

Mam said "You better tell your father because I'm not,"

She had started to calm down because he was due in from work. Dad came home but I didn't say anything to him.

Joe was great about it and said "These things happen, Irene".

When he came up later in the day he asked if I'd told my parents and I said I had told my mam and she'd been ballistic all day, then I told him what she said and his reply was:

"I wouldn't expect anything else coming from her."

I said I hadn't told my dad and didn't want to because I didn't want to hurt him.

"I'll tell him. I'll just say you are having a baby. We are engaged and plan to get married anyway so what's the difference, we'll just bring the wedding forward and get married earlier" said Joe in a matter of fact manner.

I thought it was my duty to tell my father so I plucked the courage up and said:

"Dad I have something to tell you because I can't keep it to myself anymore, mam already knows, I'm having a baby,"

Dad let out a kind of sigh and started rubbing his brow and said:

"Do you want to marry him?"

"We are engaged" I said,

"You don't have to marry him if you don't want to. We can bring the baby up as our own",

"I love him and I'm going to marry him" I said,

"Well we had better get a wedding organised" he said.

"Have you told your mam and dad?" I said to Joe,

"Uh Huh",

"What did your dad say?"

"He said tell Irene not to come to our house anymore!"

Joe was pulling my leg and started laughing. Then he said:

"My dad said, tell Irene to come down on Saturday night and we'll go to the bingo at the Ritz and see if we can win some money for the wedding. She is more than welcome here anytime."

Joe's parents, Mr & Mrs Wilson came to tea at our house and we were sat there talking and Mr Wilson said to my dad:

"I'm paying for the wedding. They can go down and see the vicar and pick a date to get married, the sooner the better."

Both Joe and I said "We don't want a big wedding just something small."

We went to see the vicar (I was from Thornley so that's where I wanted to get married) and he asked if we'd picked a date yet and we said 18 September, he looked in the diary and said 'yes we can do that date, what about 11am?', "yes that's fine", and then he must have asked a hundred questions.

He said: "When you come into church you must have the veil covering your face but you can lift it off when you say your vows."

He was a bit forthright the way he said it and sounded like an old Victorian.

At 11am on 18th September 1965 at St Bartholomew's Church in Thornley we were married and I became Irene Wilson.

I didn't get married in white but my veil was white. I had a lovely blue wedding dress which was how I wanted it. I had my sister Joan and my friend Janice as bridesmaids and Joe's brother Alfie was his best man. We had my brothers and sisters and Joe's brothers and sisters and a couple of close friends and we all went back to our house and had a tea party. What a lovely day it was.

We didn't have the pleasure of living in our own matrimonial home, we lived at my parents but it only lasted a week. Joe only had a push bike and had to bike from Thornley to Horden and back again every shift and he was exhausted the poor lad. He slept in for work twice in that first week and when we went to see his parents on the Saturday his mam said: "This is no good him cycling from village to village everyday like that, you will have to move in here with us."

We moved in and they were really lovely people. When I was getting bigger with the pregnancy, sometimes I wouldn't get out of bed until noon and Joe's dad would say:

"I don't know how you can sleep that long without wanting to go to the toilet".

On 28th March 1966 I gave birth to a healthy baby boy and called him Steven, then a year later I gave birth to another healthy child but this time it was a daughter and I called her Jayne. I went on the birth pill for some years and didn't have another baby until 1973 when we had our third and final child which was another son who we named Ian.

Steven was six months old when we got our first house, which was a lovely little two bed roomed house with front and rear garden. It was in a place called Grants Houses, which was a little mining community in between Horden and Easington Colliery. My daughter Jayne was born in that house. I loved being a mother and housewife and was content.

All my life I had looked after my siblings and parents, but I'll say this; it did put me in good stead for the life I was now living, the difference being this was mine.

I was a full-time housewife and loved every minute of it. I had a routine of housework that worked for me, and the children would be bathed and in bed by a certain time and sleep until 6am every day.

There wasn't any buses running from Grants Houses back then and we didn't have transport, so when Steven started school it was in Horden because there wasn't a school in Grants Houses.

It was hard graft taking him to school. I would push Jayne in the pram with Steven walking beside through the open fields to Horden, it was especially hard in the winter months in the snow. We were pleased when we got a three bed roomed house in Horden and were nearer to the school and the pit. Joe started work at the Horden coal mine when he left school and stayed there until it closed in 1986.

When I first walked into our new house in Horden I could feel spirit in there, it was like they had already checked it out, approved it and were waiting for our arrival. The spirit energy in that house was vibrating and it was a lovely feeling. I had never heard about spiritualism or spiritualist churches then and didn't know they even existed, that came later. If I had known then I would have gone as soon as I got the chance.

Joe had a green house in the back garden and grew lots of different vegetables and I grew lovely flowers in the front garden. Our son Ian was born in that house and the kids could play out with their friends and nobody bothered them and life was rosey. We had lots of good times and nothing but happy memories of our time there.

When Gypsy Rose said to me many years before; that I would marry someone called Joe and have three children and be happy, she was 100% correct. The Gypsy saw true.

CHAPTER 7
THE MINER'S STRIKE

I will start this chapter with an excellent poem by Mary Nightingale Bell.

THE PIT STRIKE

In nineteen eighty four,

On a chill march day,

We are on strike,

I heard the pitmen say.

My heart skipped a beat,

I thought of their wives,

Did they realise the changes,

This would bring to their lives.

No money in your purse,

A pantry that is bare,

No coal to keep you warm,

As you freeze in the cold north air.

It won't be for long,

We'll all come out,

We'll show the NCB,

Was the unions shout.

With plenty of foreign coal,

And no electricity cut,

Did any, but us care,

That the pit was shut.

Watching you search for fuel,

And worrying about bread,

The reason for the strike,

Went from my head.

I never thought that,

My heart could go on aching,

For one whole year,

Without it breaking.

At the beginning,

Your eyes were bright and clear,

As the months went by,

They were filled with fear.

Not for yourselves,

For you are the bravest of men,

But the suffering and worry,

You had brought to your kin.

I went to the town,

Saw you with your bucket,

You looked so downcast,

But you smiled as you shook it.

Calling you for begging,

The woman who passed by,

Said get to work you lazy men,

You are just work shy.

My eyes filled with tears,

As I heard this woman shout,

She did not know

What the strike was about.

I knew what you wanted,

Work for life,

Prosperity forever,

For your family and wife.

There were many others,

And I was one my friend,

Who admired your guts,

And backed you to the end.

Every day of the week,

In the busy soup kitchen,

Cooking meals and serving,

Slaved the women of Easington.

When the winter winds blew,

Station dene became bare,

Men chopped trees for their fires,

They'd grow again next year.

Christmas day came,

And then it went,

No giving or rejoicing,

It was more like lent.

I saw you go to the pit,

Looking up in despair,

At Easington pulley wheels,

So still in the air.

Your thoughts in your eyes,

Am I doing right,

Then turning back home,

To another sleepless night.

Another March day came,

A year has gone past,

The pit strike is over,

At long last.

I'll always remember,

As long as I am alive,

The end of the strike,

In nineteen eighty five.

I heard the coal trucks,

Clang on the line,

Saw the pulley wheels turn,

To take the men down the mine.

Following the banner,

Your eyes showed the pain,

As forced back to the pit,

You marched down seaside lane.

Look the world in the face,

Don't hang your head down,

For I will tell,

Of the strength of Easington.

From the first week in January until the last week in February of 1972, Miners in Great Britain went on strike over pay. It was the first strike for British miners since 1926 (although there was an unofficial strike in 1969).

They picketed power stations, ports, coal depots, steelworks and other major coal users. After a lot of negotiations between the National Union of Mineworkers and the Government, a decision was reached and the pickets were called off and the miners went back to work happy with their pay rise.

At the end of the year there was a baby boom across the country and it was blamed on the striking miners. Well, January and February have always been cold dark months haven't they!

In 1974 there was another strike over pay and Ted Heath's Conservative Government called a general election hoping to rally public support against the miners. It backfired as Heath and the Conservatives lost the election to Harold Wilson's Labour Party.

The new Labour Government offered the miners a 35% pay rise which they accepted. It was another great victory for the miners but nobody knew at the time that it would be their last and their time was numbered.

Early in 1984 the NCB (National Coal Board, which was a Government Agency), announced it would be closing twenty mines in England with the loss of around 20,000 jobs.

In March 1984 over 187,000 miners went on strike to stop the job losses and pit closures. The leader of the NUM (National Union of Mineworkers) was Arthur Scargill.

Technically the strike was illegal because there had been no national ballot by the NUM, even though some pits had called for it. Some major trade unions didn't support the NUM because of the lack of a national vote.

The Conservative Government labelled the striking miners as "the enemy within."

Prime Minister Maggie Thatcher had been importing coal in preparation and built up the coal stocks so they were plentiful (and to keep as many miners at work as possible) and she used the police (including military dressed as police) to break up the picket lines. Police on horses, in riot gear, police with dogs, picketing miners holding their ground and standing firm. There was violence and bitter disputes throughout the country in the 12 months that it lasted and miners that went to work during the strike were termed 'scabs'.

A taxi driver who was taking two 'scabs' to work died when a concrete slab was dropped from a bridge and went through his windscreen. 'Scabs' were reviled and never forgiven for betraying their community.

Women's action groups were set up and organised soup kitchens and food parcels as miners and their families were becoming poverty stricken with no money coming in and what little they had had been used.

In September 1984 the strike was ruled illegal because no national ballot had been held.

The year-long strike ended in March 1985 with victory for the Government. The miners reluctantly and bitterly voted to return to work defeated but not broken.

It was a long hard strike for the miners and their families and some of the pickets from Nottingham came up here and would picket with our lads from Horden and vice versa. The local shop keepers were brilliant and would hand out free pies and things like that.

Money wise it was a big struggle and I fell behind with the rent because there was no money coming in and others who had mortgages lost their houses. Some people actually took their own lives through it all.

The women got together and set up a soup kitchen to feed the families who needed it. When the men went out of town picketing they would be ready in the soup kitchen with a hot meal for the pickets when the bus returned. It was a close community but this brought everybody even closer and the old lady next door but one; knocked on my door and said "I hope you don't mind but here's a bag of potatoes" and I was over the moon with her generosity. People who didn't have much were helping people in need.

Lech Walesa, head of the solidarity trade union movement in Poland, sent parcels of clothing to the Horden welfare hall for the children, a lovely kind thing to do which was greatly received. Lech Walesa became President of Poland in 1990 and reigned until 1995.

My son Steven was arrested three times while out picketing. Once in Hartlepool, once in Tow Low and the other time was in Bishop Auckland. He was only young and still looked like a school kid but his face mustn't have fit and he was targeted and didn't do a thing. He didn't get charged with anything on any occasion he was arrested for nothing.

Everyone who was involved in one way or the other have their own memories of the strike, and just up the road from us at Easington Colliery, Freda Robson remembers:

"It was a hard time and we would gather wood and go to the beach to scrape up a bit of sea coal so we could at least have a fire going. I was working part time at the chemist but my low wage wasn't enough to keep us going. Luckily we got the bank to freeze the mortgage until the strike was over. We were in a huge amount of debt with not a penny to our name but at least we were fortunate enough to keep our home.

My husband Alan worked at Easington pit and one of his work mates known as John was heavily in debt. He had a wife and three children and a nice house, but as the strike was nearing its end he was so desperate and decided to go back to work and cross the picket line. He was spat on and beaten up and every window in his house was smashed. There was a lot of anger because he was giving up and letting the Tories win. The strike split the community and ripped the heart out of it.

A former work mate of mine called Mary had married a soldier and moved away down to Salisbury and they came up for a visit.

Alan and her husband Bob were talking about the strike and Alan was telling Bob about how violent the police officers had been by smashing people's heads in with truncheons and Bob just smirked and said:

"They weren't police officers they were soldiers. Maggie brought in the soldiers in police uniforms. She didn't want to lose the battle so she brought in the forces,"

Alan said "Get out of my house now!"

We never saw them again.

When you look back and think about the Tory Government, they never did like the working man. Every time the Tories came to power the working man's cost of living sky rocketed, the people with the least were always hit the hardest.

We couldn't afford to go out so we made home brew. We had some good laughs as well during the hard times especially when we had some home brew!

When the strike was nearing its end some families became estranged due to some of the lads going back to work because they had mortgages to pay and children to feed and clothe. It was turning people against people.

When it was over, the miners who didn't want to go back to work were offered redundancy and pension funds. Some went to work in factories while others moved away. The closing of the pits ripped the heart out of the mining communities and some men have never worked since. It's very sad.

At one time Horden pit employed four and a half thousand men and in May 1930 it broke the European record by mining 6,758 tons of coal in a single day! That record stood for over three decades and Horden pit finally closed in 1986.

CHAPTER 8
INTRODUCTION TO SPIRITUALISM

My husband Joe took his redundancy of £24,000 which back in 1986 was a lot of money. He paid to go on a course to become a driving instructor and that's what he did for the next 25 years. I got a job as a cleaner at Dene House Comprehensive School and I loved it. God knows I knew how to clean I had been doing it since I was a wee bairn.

After Joe became a qualified driving instructor we applied for a mortgage to buy a house. After taking all our details the man asked how long Joe had been a driving instructor and when he told him six months he replied:

"I'm sorry to tell you but you have to be self-employed for three years before you can apply for a mortgage."

We were very disappointed because we'd had our eye on a lovely house but never mind these things happen. We came out of the bank and were walking through the town centre and Joe said:

"Pick a holiday, anywhere you want to go we'll go"

There was a song playing over the tannoy system 'We're going to Barbados' and I said "Barbados,"

He said "Barbados! Irene we haven't flown before?"

"Well there's always a first time" I said.

We were on that plane for nine and a half hours and I didn't dare go to the toilet, I didn't dare walk on the plane, I didn't take my seat belt off. Every time I closed my eyes I felt like I was in a shuttle with no wheels on! I could have screamed and was glad when we finally touched down.

What a beautiful place Barbados was and we loved it. The white sandy beaches and tropical blue sea and palm trees, it was just paradise on this sun kissed Island. The people were so friendly and there was an avalanche of colours everywhere. We stayed in the parish of Christ church and one day we caught the local bus into Bridgetown which was about 15 minutes away. There was people hanging off the roof and sitting on the roof and hanging on to the sides, it was quite an experience. We watched the fisherman catch flying fish and smoke them and cook them. We drank the juice from a coconut, drank lilt, drank rum, you name it. We ate gorgeous food and drank Pina coladas until the sun went down.

We got a taxi to Harrison's cave which is a crystalized limestone cave. The calcium rich water that runs through has produced a natural wonder of stalactites and stalagmites formations. There were cascading waterfalls and natural passages; it was so beautiful I felt like I was in another world.

It was great to be waited on hand and foot for a change instead of me doing it all. What a fabulous fortnight we had and it was just the tonic we needed.

A few weeks later we got a letter off the bank and they had approved us for a mortgage! So we bought our first home after all.

We weren't there that long, only 12 months, and then we bought a shop, it was an off licence and general dealers and we lived in the flat above. I did 12 hours a day, 7 days a week in that shop for five years. It was very tying and it was running me into the ground so we sold it and moved into a Bungalow. I spent a lot of time decorating and it getting it the way I wanted it and then I got my cleaning job back at the school.

One day I was walking past a clothes shop, the same clothes shop I had walked past many times before but this day it had a notice in the window that said 'Psychic Night'. I read it and there was a guest medium called Pat Clark from Durham. Then a friend of mine saw me reading it and said "Are you going because we are" and we had a chat and I said "I don't really know, my dad always said when you're dead you're dead and you should let them rest in peace," but my friend said "Well me and our Edna are going."

I couldn't stop thinking about the Psychic night and if I should go or not but I sent a mental thought out to my spirit friends and said "I'm not making any plans but if I'm meant to be there will you get me there".

Joe went out every Friday night, if he wasn't out driving instructing he would be out down the club but this Friday night, the night of the Psychic night, for whatever reason I don't know, he wasn't working and wasn't going to the club. He was staying in!

I told him I was going out for a couple of hours to the Psychic night and wouldn't be late. I was a little nervous about going and spoke to my grandma in my mind and asked her to look after me. My daughter Jayne came with me and I got the shock of my life when I went in because I saw people who I knew and one of the organisers said "It's lovely to see you here Irene". It was nothing like I had imagined.

When the medium came on she gave a few messages and then pointed to me and said:

"Can I speak to the lady in the spotted blouse sitting next to the radiator?"

"Me?" I said shocked,

"Yes, You," was her reply.

She gave me some amazing messages, one was off Joe's dad who said he had left a watch and was a miner (all true), another off my grandma and the medium described her to a tee and there was one for my dad off he's old friend Travis. I had never even heard of Travis. Little did I know but he was my dad's best friend at school and dad's best man at his wedding. Travis took his own life age 18 at Corkys pond in Thornley before I was born. When I passed Travis' message on to dad he was blown away.

I said to dad: "You know something dad. I have never disagreed with you or mam and have never back chatted any of you. You have always said to me when you're dead you're dead, let them rest. Well last night what that lady said to me has proven that there is something else and the spirit people I have seen since childhood has not been my imagination."

That was my introduction to spiritualism and that lady didn't just give messages from loved ones, she gave evidence that life goes on somewhere else in another world on a higher vibration. I came out of there walking on air. I wish I'd have known about Spiritualism when I was younger. I knew this was what I wanted to do. I knew I had been with spirit since I was four years old and it took a medium to open my eyes to the fact, and she said I was already working with spirit which I was really.

I think it was the start of the motions of what I was going to step into, a new journey, although it had always been with me. I started going regular to the spiritualist church and every time

I walked through the door I felt like I had 'came home' if want of a better word. I thoroughly enjoyed sitting in the congregation every week and watching a different medium give messages from the so called dead. I noticed every medium worked differently, they all had their own way of delivering the messages. I found out there was an open circle once a week were people could develop their psychic abilities if they had any. I started going to the open circle and one week a well-established medium told me that I should stand up and give off what I get because spirit are with me and I will be a good medium. I also started reading books about spirit and getting a little more knowledge on the subject. I also went to other open circles with my daughter and her friend and I gave lots of messages and I was growing in confidence.

One night in the open circle I heard a voice behind me shout 'Christine' and I stood up, I felt like I was getting pushed off my chair to stand up. I said "All I can here is a lady's voice saying 'Christine' and then I heard 'That's the one' and I was directed to a young lady who was sitting there. I said "Can you take the name Christine?" and she said "I am Christine." I was pretty shocked but when she acknowledged it everything else started to come through. Her grandma came through with a baby that had been born here but wasn't here very long before going to spirit and Christine said 'Yes'. Everything else I told her she said yes to. Then I saw an old bus with the word Wales on it. I was hearing the voice and seeing the vision in front of my eyes. I described everything I was seeing and saw a man driving a bus through the Welsh mountains and through the winding roads and he was wearing a cap and a badge. She said "My granda was a bus driver in Wales and that's where I've just moved from."

After I gave my first message I went to the toilet and said to myself 'yes' and was pretty excited about what had just happened. I went back in and after the open circle had finished everybody was saying 'well done' to me. It made me realise that all the experiences I'd had with spirit since I was a child was that they were there for a reason.

I went to the open circle every week and each week I gave messages off, I could see spirit and hear spirit and felt very privileged to be able to do so.

One week during a questions and answers session another girl called Christine said that she was working in a shop that her sister had bought, it was being renovated and things were happening like there was a spirit in there. While she was saying this I closed my eyes and heard a man's voice say "Tell her it's me and my name is Walter," so I stood up and walked over to her and said:

"I've got a gentleman here and he is telling me that his name is Walter,"

Christine's mouth dropped open with a shock on her face and she said:

"That was the man who had the shop before my sister and he died. There are walls being knocked down and it's getting modernised,"

Then Walter spoke fluently to me and said he didn't like what they were doing to his beloved shop and liked it the way it was when he had it etc, and I relayed everything to Christine who said "Yes but we have to do it." I said "Yes you have to because it needs to be done but you have been hearing and sensing things in the shop and now you know who it is. It is

Walter and he isn't happy that the shop is being modernised because he likes it the way it was. It is just conformation to you that there is someone there."

What spiritualism does is it removes the fear of death, comforts the bereaved, gives new hope to the lonely and forsaken, gives healing to the sick and demonstrates the truth of survival and communication after the death of the physical body.

CHAPTER 9
THE MEDIUM

A medium is a person who can receive and relay information from the mind of a discarnate person. This is achieved by the use of psychic faculties, found to some extent in everybody, but capable of being developed in the case of the medium, to a high pitch of sensitivity by training and meditation.

I would sit quiet after I had got the Sunday dinner over with and link in with spirit. They would tell me I am the one who is in control of what comes out of my mouth, which I didn't know then is what we call personal responsibility. When you got into spiritualism and it became a way of life you learned the 'seven principles' and tried to live your life that way as best as you could and personal responsibility is principle number five, I'll talk later about them.

The more you drive a car the better driver you become and it's the same with mediumship. The more you link and work with spirit the better medium you become. I had been giving messages week in and week out at the open circle for around four years and one day the phone rang and on the other end was a lady from Gateshead.

"Irene do you do services?" she said,

"No"

"Well you should because I was at the open circle on Thursday and I saw you giving messages and you are very good," she said,

"I've never took a service before," said I,

"You know what, there is always the first time," she said.

For some reason I said yes I'll take the service at Gateshead. A service consists of two parts, the first part the medium gives philosophy and the second part is the demonstration of clairvoyance.

On my way to Gateshead my stomach was turning over and my knees were knocking, I was a bag of nerves. My nervousness wasn't helped when I walked through the doors and the place was packed out!

I silently said to spirit "You orchestrated it for me to be here and now I'm here so please don't leave me."

My philosophy was about the Fox sisters who started the spiritualist movement in the 1840s and spirit were also feeding me things to say. When the philosophy was over everybody clapped and I knew it had went well. I recall I gave some evidential messages during the clairvoyance because after it everyone stood up and clapped again. One message stands out even though it was a little uncomfortable.

Four young lads were sat at the back and I went to one of them because spirit was in my ear saying "Tell him Josephine, talk about Josephine,"

I pointed to one of the lads and told him and I'd like to come to him and asked him if he knew a Josephine who was still living?

He looked at his mates and they all laughed. I brought his grandma through who said she was watching over him etc and I said "I keep getting Josephine; you must know a Josephine",

He said he didn't know anyone called Josephine but he knew what I was talking about and wanted to see me in private and I said ok. Then I said "You want to grow your hair long so you can tie it back and put it in a pony-tail and things like that,"

"Yes I do" he said.

Then spirit said to me "It's a girl," so I said "I can hear it's a girl, is it a baby?"

He said "No"

Then spirit told me there was a transition coming around him. I still didn't click on because when they said transition I thought they meant he was going to die.

"I know where you are coming from just leave the message for now and I'll see you after the service." He said.

I think everyone in the audience knew what the message was about apart from me. The penny didn't drop until he came to see me after the service.

"My name is Joe" he said,

"Hello Joe, my husband is called Joe",

"I'm not going to be Joe for much longer. I'm going to London next week for a big operation. I'm going to be Josephine" he said.

When I got home I said to spirit "Why did you give me that. Why?"

I felt a little embarrassed but didn't realise until later that when you work with spirit you become more humble and empathetic. I am only the messenger and a channel for spirit to work through. After that service my phone never stopped ringing for bookings and my diary was full.

"Because you are a spirit you survive death and because you are a spirit you are alive today. The spirit within you, which causes you to live, is the same spirit that animates every member of every nation, of every race, creed and colour.

Spiritually, the people of the world are one. Spiritualism reveals the spiritual oneness of all mankind. God has made us all members of one vast spiritual family." Maurice Barbanell

I was heavily involved with my local spiritualist church for years, I went on the committee for a while as membership secretary, then booking secretary and a little later I became president, a position I held for about five years before I left to do my own thing. The reason I left to do my own thing was because I had befriended a few women and introduced them to the church and they became members. My so called friends seen the position I was in and wanted what I had so I left them all to it.

I opened an open circle once a week in the welfare hall and I was getting 90 people through the doors such was my reputation, it was packed every week. I was doing that for a while and I asked spirit to find me a place so I could open my own independent spiritualist church and as I was going home one week from the open circle I seen a 'To Let' sign with a phone number on so I gave it a ring. We met the next day and had a look around and took it on and we got to work cleaning and painting and getting everything just right.

Every day when we opened the door during that week there would be feathers on the floor. My friend Ann said there must be pigeons in the loft but we could never hear anything. I got a builder out to do a little work and asked him if he thought we had pigeons in the loft. He said "No, what makes you think that," and I said "Because every time we come in here there are feathers on the floor."

He checked the loft out and said it was clear and there wasn't anything in it.

We got a rostrum built, carpeted the place out and got plenty of tables and chairs and everything else fell into place.

When I opened my own spiritualist church in Sixth Street, Horden, it was packed every week.

It wasn't plain sailing because there was a lot of hard work involved but we knew we had spirit on our side.

Monday we have healing. Wednesday is the open circle. Saturday is the development class and Sunday is the divine service where the visiting medium gives philosophy and a demonstration of clairvoyance.

We do a 12 week awareness class to start off with to bring your awareness out. Then after that you start the development class which is very good and pretty intense and it's nice to see the student's progress come on leaps and bounds.

People who wish to unfold their mediumistic potential or just wish to learn more about the science and philosophy of spiritualism should enrol on a course or teaching class.

Do you believe in Heaven and Hell and if you do what do you think they are? Do you want to know what they really are? They are states of mind brought about by right or wrong thought and action. They are not places to which we are sent by a God who judges us. We reap what we sow.

When I was younger I didn't like doing the philosophy but I got used to it when I made a stronger connection with my guide who helps me with it. I would feel like I was going smaller because my guide for philosophy is Chinese.

Spirit say names are not important but I named him Confucius to get an understanding of who he was and what his workings where. He is a lovely philosophist and also has a sense of humour. He once said "He who makes love on bankside is not on the level" which made me have a fit of giggles. He has some funny sayings but that's just his character.

Philosophy is usually neglected by the average person and difficult to understand. It seems too speculative for most. If one could say that it is possible to get confirmation of a 'real' world underlying our earthly experience, it could boost idealist philosophy from speculative to factual knowledge. If anyone asked me if I believe in life after death I'd say I don't 'believe', I 'know', there is a difference in 'believing' and 'knowing'.

Sometimes when I meditate and I just want peace to come around me there is a lovely Monk who draws close, he is quite chunky and when he overshadows me I feel like a bullfrog!

When I first heard the word meditation I thought you sat in a yoga position and chanted the OM word! How wrong I was. Certain people throughout the world do it but we don't. Meditation is a concentrated focus and the more you practice, the more you are able to get into the flow of a universal life force. There are many forms of meditation which do not require the total stillness of the body. Painting, writing, gardening, dancing, exercise, are forms of meditation if you find it therapeutic. To me they are another way of opening up our minds and whenever we tune into the creative force within ourselves, we are in essence meditating.

The meditation for opening up to spirit is sitting in a comfortable chair with no distractions, TV turned off, phone switched off or unplugged, sitting upright with your feet on the ground, spine straight to allow the energies to flow more easily. Palms of your hands on your thighs and once you are in a relaxed position you concentrate on your breathing. The key is slow relaxed deep breaths in from the midsection and slow exhales out. After you have sat for a while in meditation it will get better and become easier. I won't go into it here this is just a very brief explanation. Meditation is also great to de-stress after a hectic day.

CHAPTER 10
THE SEVEN PRINCIPLES

The seven principles were given through the trance mediumship of Emma Harding Britten in 1871.

Emma was an advocate of the early modern spiritualist movement. She was known for inspirational writings and addresses which were very informative and inspiring.

She travelled throughout England, America, Canada, Australia and New Zealand giving lectures and trance demonstrations to packed out theatres in the late 1800s.

Born in 1823 in London, as a child she often saw dead family friends and relatives, as well as being able to predict the outcome of coming events.

Emma passed to spirit in Manchester in 1899 age 66.

When I became a spiritualist many years ago and learned about the seven principles and have tried to live my life in accordance with them.

THE SEVEN PRINCIPLES

1 THE FATHERHOOD OF GOD

2 THE BROTHERHOOD OF MAN

3 THE COMMUNION OF SPIRITS AND THE MINISTRY OF ANGELS

4 THE CONTINUOUS EXISTENCE OF THE HUMAN SOUL

5 PERSONAL RESPONSIBILITY

6 COMPENSATION AND RETRIBUTION HEREAFTER FOR ALL THE GOOD AND EVIL DEEDS DONE ON EARTH

7 ETERNAL PROGRESS OPEN TO EVERY HUMAN SOUL

Here are some interpretations of the seven principles of spiritualism.

The Fatherhood of God:

God, the father; the creator; the universal energy; this power we call God is within us all.

God created all life and so is spoken of as the father.

The Brotherhood of Man:

In accepting God as the father, we accept that we are all God's children so therefore we are all brothers and sisters in one universal family.

As spiritualists we try to understand the needs of others regardless of race, creed and colour.

The Communion of Spirits and the Ministry of Angels:

When a medium communicates with people in spirit to provide factual evidence that supports our philosophy.

There is nothing supernatural about it. It is a natural process, a normal activity.

The Ministry of Angels brings enhanced wisdom to enlighten the individual and the world we live in.

Continuous Existence of the Human Soul:

Energy cannot be destroyed it can only change its form. When the physical body dies the spirit continues to live in a different dimension with the same personality and characteristics.

You can't die for the life of you!

Personal Responsibility:

What each of us makes of our lives is our personal responsibility. No one can save us from our wrong doings but ourselves.

As we are given freedom of choice or fee will, we are also given the ability to recognise what is right from what is wrong.

We are totally, as well as personally, responsible.

Compensation and Retribution Hereafter for all the Good and Evil Deeds done on Earth:

Actions create results according to natural law. As you sow, so shall you reap.

One cannot be cruel to others and expect love and popularity in return. The law of cause and effect comes to mind.

It must be understood that compensatory and retributive effects of this law apply now on earth. They do not wait until we begin to live in the spirit world.

Eternal Progress Open To Every Human Soul:

Eternity does not begin at death; progress is open to all now!

Any action, or intent to change, to promote soul growth and progression, creates a positive reaction. There is always an opportunity to develop and move forward.

CHAPTER 11
BACK FROM THE DEAD

I used to go to see my parents on a Saturday for an hour but when my dad passed away I stopped going. My dad woke up one morning and shouted for my mam who was in the kitchen and when she went upstairs he was dead in bed, he was 73. It was a sad time for me because I loved my dad and thought the world of him.

Mam was 85 when she passed away but it wasn't the same with her because of how she treated me. I loved her because she was my mam but that was all, we never had a good relationship. She was very poorly in hospital and I went to see her. She couldn't eat or drink or open her eyes and her body was shutting down. Our Joan said "Mam our Irene is here to see you" and she never moved and then Joan repeated it louder "Mam our Irene is here to see you" and a few seconds later her eyes opened wide and she said "I'm sorry" and closed her eyes. Her words didn't mean anything to me because I'd learned to harden myself to them over the years, so I replied "You've got nothing to be sorry about" and turned away. Mam died soon after.

One day my daughter, who was a teachers helper at the local junior school, asked if I would do a fundraiser for the school to get disco lights and things so I said yes but a couple of my medium friends Bill and Shirley gave clairvoyance as well and we raised £520 which was greatly received.

I think I must have got bit by the fundraising bug because I did loads of clairvoyant nights and raised money for various charities like £500 for Mencap, £2000 for Durham St Johns Ambulance, £1000 for Cotsford School, £14,30 for Pakistan Earthquake appeal, £500 for Alzheimer's Centre, £1,100 for Haemorrhage Foundation, £500 for chemotherapy unit, £500 for Macmillan cancer support, £1,700 for the Great North Air

Ambulance, £800 for Hartlepool Hospice, we raised money for a young girl to go to ballet school, just about everything really the list goes on and on. It was great to be of service. I didn't do it on my own as various medium friends helped me like John Knox and Peter Crawford and we all played our part.

There has also been the odd newspaper story or two like the following edited version:

When Irene Wilson was five years old she began to start seeing and feeling spirits. Talking to the dead is a way of life.

"I have always been spiritual since I was little. But the spiritualist church allowed it to come out. I was brought up a Protestant and went to a Methodist church where I followed the Ten Commandments. It was only when I started going to the spiritualist church that I found out it wasn't like that. Spiritualism lets you know who you are, what your purpose is and what you do when you leave this place. This is your physical life and when you pass away your spirit goes into a spiritual world.

We are a go between with spirits and people who are still here. It is more fun having another medium with you to do a demonstration of clairvoyance especially when we are raising money for charity. The audience like seeing how the clairvoyants work together and sometimes we are able to give out phone numbers and addresses to prove there is someone out there. Spiritualism is about having a gift and sharing it with other people to help those less fortunate. It brings a lot of comfort and reassurance to people. It is an uplifting feeling for you to go to people and bring that evidence through for them and let them know that their loved ones have just gone to another dimension. It is like a rush of adrenaline when you begin to feel spirit draw close. My great grandma was also a medium. It is not just a hobby it's a way of life."

'Irene has raised over £50,000 for various charities. A part time cleaning supervisor, her charity events are held in conjunction with Peter Crawford, who regularly sees lawyers, accountants and teachers who need his help.'

A few years ago my eyes became really sore and I was having a lot of trouble with them. I thought I needed new glasses so I went for an eye test. During the test I couldn't read anything and couldn't really see anything. I was sent to Sunderland eye infirmary and was told I had cataracts on both eyes but my eyes were too dry to operate on so I was given eye drops. Then I went to Newcastle RVI and had tests done which all came back clear. I was as blind as a bat and couldn't see anything, everything was just a blur.

Eventually I got my right eye operated on and about a month later my left eye was also fixed, although I had a small tear in the corner through rubbing it with dry eye syndrome.

I started losing weight which I thought was good at first but then I started to lose too much and everything became an effort and I had no energy. I got a chest and throat infection which made things ten times worse. I felt like I was having a meltdown because I had been doing too much and it was taking its toll on me. People had been telling me for long enough to slow down but I didn't listen. I should have rested when my body told me to but I ignored it and then I went to bed and was too weak to get up and was there for three weeks.

I got rushed into Sunderland General Hospital and they put 15 and a half bags of fluid into me because I was severely dehydrated. I don't think they realised how ill I was until the next day, I couldn't feed myself, wash myself and couldn't lift my arms up I was so weak.

24 hours after being rushed in I lost consciousness and knew I was at death's door. There were three steps and a door in front of me so I walked up them and knocked on the door and they wouldn't let me in! Then an invisible force turned me around and I was looking at two doors, one door was for healing and the other door had different rooms going off it. I chose that door and walked along the corridor and saw an old friend called Linda who had died a few years previous.

"Hello Irene would you like to come and see my room" she said, so I went in and the room was half papered red which was her favourite colour.

I said "Why have you only half papered your room" and she replied "Because I'm waiting for my husband to choose his colour when he comes over." That is all I recall of the conversation.

Then I remember the doctor at my bedside saying "Come back Irene, come on, come back, we need you here," and I opened my eyes and I was back. I was back from the dead!

I was given antibiotics through a drip and fluids and I just slept like a log most of the time.

I got a cat-scan and ultra sound scan and the surgeon said to me: "I've just looked at your doctor's records and I can't believe you have never been to the doctors in the last 25 years!"

"You've got a chest infection and a throat infection and it's caused your gall bladder to inflame but you haven't got gall stones." He said.

I was in that hospital bed for a week and didn't move and then I was sent home. The illness took its toll on me and took me a long time to recover from and I hated being away from my beloved little spiritualist church. It was eight months before I walked back through them doors and in that time there was still rent to pay and also gas, electricity and water rates. My friends were there when I needed them and ran things as normal without me. Linzi, Phillip, Julie, Joan and Alice rolled their sleeves up and all mucked in. Connie and Jimmy kept the open circle going. The place would have shut if it wasn't for all of them and I can't thank them enough.

When I returned after eight months I was still weak and had to take things easy, just fairy steps to begin with. I'm not as bouncy as I was but I'm not as young as I was either. I'm gradually getting stronger day by day and am doing services again and back to running my church, Spiritualist Friendship Centre in Horden. I love that place it's my little piece of heaven.

Spirit where there for me when I was young and I will always be there for them.

I eat, live and breathe spirit.

Everything I have told you in this book is the truth, the whole truth and nothing but the truth.

I hope you enjoyed reading my journey.

God bless you all. Irene xx

Also available from Warcry Press

Northern Warrior

by Richy Horsley

ISBN: 978-1-912543-01-4

30 Years a Fighter

'The Fighting Memoirs of Kevin 'Bulldog' Bennett'

Richy Horsley with Kevin Bennett

ISBN: 978-1-912543-09-0

Battling Bowes

by Richy Horsley

ISBN: 978-1-912543-08-3